P9-APJ-831

Pilotless Planes

by Carla Mooney

NORWOODHOUSE PRESS

Norwood House Press
PO Box 316598
Chicago, Illinois 60631

For information regarding Norwood House Press, please visit our Web site at:

www.norwoodhousepress.com or call 866-565-2900.

© 2011 by Norwood House Press.

All rights reserved.

No part of this book may be reproduced without written permission from the publisher.

LIBRARY OF CONGRESS CATALOGING-IN-PUBLICATION DATA

Mooney, Carla, 1970–
  Pilotless planes / Carla Mooney.
    p. cm. — (A great idea)
  Includes bibliographical references and index.
  Summary: "Pilotless Planes" or "drones" have become an important aspect of
modern military operations. Developed for espionage and warfare, pilotless
planes are also used for public safety issues and can reduce injury or death
rates for pilots"—Provided by publisher.
  ISBN-13: 978-1-59953-381-0 (library edition : alk. paper)
  ISBN-10: 1-59953-381-2 (library edition : alk. paper)
  1. Drone aircraft—Juvenile literature. 2. Uninhabited combat aerial
vehicles—Juvenile literature. I. Title.
  UG1242.D7M66 2010
  623.74'69—dc22
                                                                    2010008500

Manufactured in the United States of America in North Mankato, Minnesota.
164N–072010

RD431166930

Contents

Chapter 1:
Spies in the Sky   4

Chapter 2:
Flying Pilotless: How It Works   15

Chapter 3:
UAVs: Making a Difference   26

Chapter 4:
Taking Off in the Future   35

Glossary   45

For More Information   46

Index   47

Picture Credits   48

About the Author   48

Note: Words that are **bolded** in the text are defined in the glossary on page 45.

Spies in the Sky

It is 3 A.M. A solitary man slowly appears in the quiet, dark night. He walks up a street and enters a building. The man must think he is alone in the darkness. Unknown to him, however, watchful eyes follow his every move.

Eleven thousand feet (3,343m) above, a Predator **drone** circles in the sky. The plane is too small and too high for anyone on the ground to hear or see it. The drone carries an **infrared** camera. It films everything it sees from the camera mounted in its nose.

The drone's pilot has orders to look for any enemy movement in the area. He has been watching the building for almost four hours, looking for anything that seems unusual or out of place. The man's movements in the middle of the night appear suspicious. The pilot settles in to watch and wait. From high above, the drone's watchful eye may discover information tonight that leads to hidden weapons or an enemy camp.

The pilot, however, is not in the plane. Instead, he sits in front of a computer screen and watches a video in a trailer more

An air force pilot on the ground views information sent by a UAV as it flies over a battlefield thousands of miles away.

? **Did You Know?**

The first aerial spies used in **combat** were hot air balloons flown over Civil War battlefields.

than 7,000 miles (11,265km) away. Using a **satellite**, computers and a joystick, he flies the pilotless plane by remote control.

What Is a UAV?

A new weapon sometimes changes the rules of battle during a war. The Predator is such a war-changing weapon. It is an unmanned aerial vehicle (UAV). These planes have become very important to the U.S. Air

Predators carry two Hellfire missiles, like the one shown here, as part of their weapons package.

Force. Dozens flew over war zones in Iraq and Afghanistan, 24 hours a day.

UAVs fly without anyone on board. That is why they are sometimes called pilotless planes. Despite the name, UAVs do have pilots. Yet instead of being in the plane, the pilots fly UAVs from a ground station that can be thousands of miles away. They use remote controls to tell the plane what to do. Be-

cause the pilot is not on board, the plane can fly on the most dangerous missions. If

Target Drones

Planes were first used in combat during World War I. By World War II the first pilotless aerial vehicles appeared. They were not spy planes, however. Instead soldiers used them for training exercises. They fired weapons at the target drones to learn how to shoot at airplanes. Because drones did not have pilots, no one was hurt. This generation of UAVs was more like remote-controlled toys than military weapons.

The KDD, or Katydid, was the U.S. Navy's first jet-propelled pilotless target drone.

An MQ-1B Predator pilotless aircraft flies over the Nevada desert during a training exercise.

the plane goes down, the pilot stays safe at the ground station.

A pilotless plane like the Predator is lighter than a traditional plane. Because a lighter plane uses less fuel, it can fly over enemy land for a long time. This makes it good for **surveillance** missions. The plane's cameras take photos and videos. They can also record radio conversations. Using a satellite link, the UAV sends its pictures and videos to military commanders. There is almost no time delay in receiving the pictures or videos. Commanders see the events on the ground while they are happening.

Some UAVs are more than flying spies. These pilotless planes also carry weapons. First they use their cameras to find and identify a target. Then commanders can remotely launch missiles or drop bombs from the UAV to attack the targets on the ground.

The Need for UAVs

During a war it is important for military commanders to know what the enemy is doing. Where is its base? How many soldiers does it have? Is the enemy moving to attack? What weapons does it have? These are all questions that commanders want to answer. For centuries commanders have used spies to gather this information.

UAVs Take Flight

Military commanders knew that using pilotless planes on dangerous spy missions would save the lives of pilots. During the Vietnam War the U.S. Air Force developed a pilotless plane called the Lightning Bug. It used the Lightning Bug to fly into dangerous places where it did not want to risk pilots' lives. Another plane launched the Lightning Bug. Once it was launched, the Lightning Bug took pictures of targets. When it was done, a helicopter picked the Bug up. The Lightning Bug's early navigation and computer systems often did not work correctly. Many times the plane missed its target and returned with no useful film.

During the 1980s the United States built another UAV called the Pioneer. It

Israeli Innovations

During the 1970s, Israel built small UAVs that were the size of large model airplanes. These UAVs carried inexpensive, lightweight video cameras. When Israel went to war with Syria in 1982, pilots operated the UAVs with remote controls. They flew over the Bekaa Valley and spotted more than two dozen Syrian antiaircraft sites. Their information helped the Israelis destroy their enemy sites. The Israelis were then able to shoot down up to 100 jets without any Israeli losses. The Israelis also used their UAVs to support ground troops. The Israeli success renewed interest in UAVs around the world. In fact, the Predator is based on an Israeli UAV design.

held a powerful video camera and could fly for hours at a time. The Pioneer's first combat action came during the Gulf War.

It helped U.S. Navy gunners bombard targets. The Pioneer flew over the targets and sent video to the gunners' computer screens. The gunners used the video to see where their shells had landed. They knew if they had hit their target or if they had to fire again. The Pioneer's video told them if they needed to adjust their aim. It was real-time battle information.

Although the Pioneer was useful, it had drawbacks. To land, the Pioneer had to fly into a net hung above the battleship's deck.

The U.S. military used the very first Pioneer UAVs for **reconnaissance** and artillery spotting during the Gulf War in Iraq. Here, mechanics work on the aircraft.

? Did You Know?

The Predator is a relatively slow plane. Its top speed is only 135 miles per hour (217km/h). In comparison, a typical commercial jet airliner has a cruising speed of about 500 to 600 miles per hour (800 to 960km/h).

Many times the landing damaged the plane and it needed repairs. In addition, the plane was noisy. Its engine sounded like a lawnmower flying in the sky. The enemy quickly realized that if it heard that sound, fire from battleships would soon follow.

The Pioneer was also limited in how far it could fly. Pilots controlled the plane with radio signals from a ground station. To send those signals, the station had to keep a line-of-sight link with the plane. That meant the UAV could not fly too far from the station. When the UAV flew over the horizon, the curve of the earth broke the link. Sometimes geography, such as mountains, broke the link. Other times weather conditions or equipment failures interrupted the radio link. When that happened the pilots could no longer control the UAV. The plane might crash or fly out of control.

Flying Longer and Farther

In 1993 the U.S. Department of Defense put out a call for new UAVs. It wanted a pilotless plane that could fly longer and farther. One company, General Atomics Aeronautical Systems, Incorporated (GA-ASI), quickly began work on a new model called the Predator. A snowmobile engine powered the plane. GA-ASI installed traffic helicopter cameras in the plane. It also gave the Predator a propeller instead of jets. This would let the plane remain almost stationary in the air. GA-ASI loaded the Predator with the latest computers and digital data storage. The Predator also used global positioning satellites to help it navigate. Now the UAV could be connected to controllers thousands of miles away. In 1995 the Predator saw its first combat action in the Balkans. The Predator planes flew more than 600 U.S. Air Force missions in their first year.

The Predator solved many of the problems the earlier UAVs had. This small plane was only 27 feet (8m) long, about 10 feet (3m) shorter than the average school bus. It could fly for 24 hours over an area that was 460 miles (740km) away from the airfield before it needed to refuel. It could

Assisted by a pilot on the ground, a Pioneer UAV comes in for a landing.

The Predator has special design features that make it lighter than the Pioneer UAV.

also fly at an altitude of 25,000 feet (7,620m) using a quieter engine. At that level it was almost impossible to see or hear from the ground. Its satellite links allowed operators to stay in contact and control the plane from greater distances. For the first time, commanders in the United States could watch a television screen that showed what was happening on the ground in the Middle East.

Today's Predator carries high-powered zoom cameras, infrared sensors, and radar. It takes pictures and video during the day or night. Unlike satellites, the Predator can fly underneath cloud cover and take pictures in any type of weather. The Predator's cameras are powerful. They can show a person's facial features from 5 miles (8km) in the air. That is as high as 88 football fields stacked end to end into the sky!

The Corona Spy Satellite

In addition to planes, the United States used the Corona satellite during the Cold War to spy on enemies. As it orbited Earth, the satellite took pictures above target areas. To deliver its film, the satellite ejected the film capsule in a bucketlike container with a parachute. A catcher plane flew to grab it and reel in the film. One drawback was that the Corona's information was old by the time intelligence experts looked at it. In addition, satellites like the Corona moved quickly over Earth's surface. The satellite took pictures and then continued its orbit. It could take hours or days before the satellite returned to the same spot and took another picture. The enemy could constantly move troops and weapons to hide from the satellite.

Shown here is a U.S. spy satellite photograph of a military base in the former Soviet Union during the Cold War.

Another important tool on the Predator is called a laser designator. Controllers use the laser to mark targets. When another aircraft fires a missile, the laser guides the missile to the target. By 2000 the Predator was able to hold its own weapons. It now carries and fires laser-guided Hellfire missiles. The armed Predator has become one of the military's most efficient weapons. It can find, identify, and destroy a target in seconds.

Since 2001, the United States has regularly used pilotless planes. UAVs give the U.S. military an advantage during combat. That is why ground commanders like them. Several different models of UAVs are in use, including the Reaper and the Global Hawk. The Predator, however, remains the most widely used. As of 2009, the U.S. Air Force had flown Predators more than 650,000 flight hours. The Predator has supported ground troops in Iraq, Afghanistan, and around the world, and it has become the most battle-proven UAV to date.

Chapter 2

Flying Pilotless: How It Works

GA-ASI, the San Diego company that developed the Predator, works to build and improve pilotless planes. It uses the latest **avionics**, electronics, and satellites to fly its UAVs.

Improved Endurance

A plane's endurance is its ability to stay in flight for a long time. Endurance is a key advantage that the Predator has over piloted planes for surveillance missions. Jets and satellites can only glimpse a target as they pass over it. Pilotless planes can linger and watch a target for 24 hours or longer.

The Predator has long endurance because it is not limited by carrying a pilot. It therefore does not need to land to give the pilot a break for food or rest. The Predator also does not carry the weight of a pilot, seats, control instruments, and oxygen systems. Without this extra weight, this UAV

More fuel-efficient than manned planes, the MQ-1B Predator can hover over a target for hours.

is smaller and lighter than a piloted plane. In fact, a Predator weighs about 1,130 pounds (513kg). That is only 40 percent of the weight of a Volkswagen Beetle! Lighter planes do not burn as much fuel in the air. This allows the Predator to re-main in flight for 24 hours on only one tank of gas.

A Strong-as-Steel Fabric

Another reason why the Predator is so light is because it is made of fabric! GA-ASI uses rolls of black carbon fiber or graphite fabrics to build the Predator. Before cutting, these fabrics are filled with **epoxy resin**. The thin black cloth is about 30 times stronger than steel. The GA-ASI workers use machines to cut the fabric in predesigned patterns. Then they layer the cut fabric over metal or plastic molds. The molds give shape to the fabric pieces. Each piece becomes a different part of the plane, such as a wing or landing gear. The workers also use small spacers between fabric layers. The honeycomb pattern in a piece of cardboard uses a similar idea. The small spaces between layers add strength, but not weight, to each piece.

After the fabric pieces are set on their molds, they are heated and cured in a 250°F (121°C) oven. The heat triggers a chemical reaction in the epoxy resin. It binds the fabrics together and hardens them in the mold's shape. The process is like heating a piece of cloth that is coated with glue. The heat dries the glue and makes the cloth hard. The resulting parts are as strong as steel but are much lighter.

Next each piece is trimmed. The workers then assemble and paint the Predator. Workers also install the engine and electronic equipment. In a final step, the plane's wings are attached to the body.

Easy to Transport

One great thing about the Predator system is that it is easy to transport. The plane breaks down into six pieces that fit in a large crate. The crew loads the crates, the ground control station trailer, and a large satellite antenna on a cargo plane. The Predator system is then ready to be delivered anywhere in the world.

In Nevada, members of the 757th Aircraft Maintenance Squadron pack a pilotless Predator for shipment to Afghanistan.

Eyes in the Sky

GA-ASI designed the Predator to carry cameras for spying. Three high-powered zoom cameras sit in a compartment below the Predator's nose. Two color video cameras record images in daylight. An infrared camera sees images during low-light or night missions. The infrared camera measures heat changes between objects that other cameras cannot see at night. In addition, two high-powered zoom color and infrared cameras sit in the plane's

The Predator is equipped with an infrared imaging sensor, left, and a "heads up" pilot display, below, that shows in great detail what the plane's camera is seeing on the ground.

nose. The pilot uses the view from the nose cameras to help fly the plane.

The Predator is also equipped with synthetic aperture radar (SAR). Whereas cameras use light to create an image, SAR uses radar signals. This allows it to create images in complete darkness. SAR also sees through rain, clouds, and snow.

As the UAV flies, its SAR antenna sends out pulses of high-frequency radar waves. The radar waves bounce off objects on the ground and travel back to the SAR antenna. Each bounced, or backscatter, wave carries information. The time it takes to bounce back tells how far away the object is. The backscatter waves also tell the computer about the object. Trees absorb the signal's energy and appear grey. Metal objects reflect most of the en-

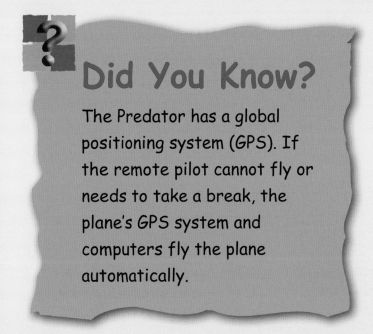

Did You Know?

The Predator has a global positioning system (GPS). If the remote pilot cannot fly or needs to take a break, the plane's GPS system and computers fly the plane automatically.

ergy back and appear brighter. A computer stores the data from the backscatter waves. It performs millions of calculations and looks for patterns. The computer uses these patterns to create photolike images that **intelligence analysts** see on-screen.

Staying Connected to a Team of Operators

Predators may not have a pilot on board, but many people on the ground control them. One set of pilots and operators are at a ground station that is close to where the plane will fly. This crew maintains the Predator planes. It makes any repairs or adjustments needed after each mission. It also loads missiles onto the plane.

During a mission this nearby crew handles the Predator's takeoff. It uses radio signals to launch the plane and control it in the air. The signals travel in a straight line from the ground crew's transmitter to the UAV's receiver. For the line-of-sight link to work, nothing can block it. The link also has a very short range and only works for about 170 miles (274km). Once the plane is several thousand feet in the air, the crew uses a satellite link to hand off the plane's control to the mission team.

The Predator uses a two-person mission team. A pilot "flies" the plane. A sensor operator works the Predator's cameras and sensors. Unlike the nearby crew, the mission team can control the Predator from thousands of miles away.

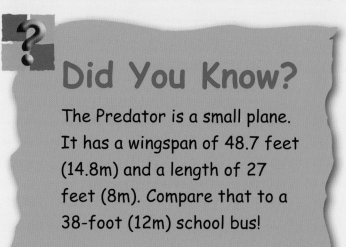

Did You Know?

The Predator is a small plane. It has a wingspan of 48.7 feet (14.8m) and a length of 27 feet (8m). Compare that to a 38-foot (12m) school bus!

Global Hawk

The Global Hawk is the largest UAV built to date. It has a 131-foot-long (40m) wingspan and can carry 3,000 pounds (1,361kg) of equipment. The Global Hawk soars as high as 65,000 feet (19,812m). Flying so high makes it hard for the enemy to shoot it down. It also allows the Global Hawk to watch a much wider area of the ground than other UAVs. Unlike the Predator, the Global Hawk does not need a ground pilot. The plane is programmed to fly itself from takeoff to landing. Operators on the ground monitor the plane while it is in the air. The Global Hawk can stay in the air for as long as 35 hours at a time. With this endurance the Global Hawk is perfect for long surveillance missions.

A Global Hawk surveys large areas of land with pinpoint accuracy.

When the Predator flew over Afghanistan or Iraq, the mission team often worked from an air base in the United States. To stay connected, the mission team used a satellite link to send and receive signals. First the mission team sent commands to a satellite. The satellite then redirected the signals to a receiver on the plane. The satellite also relayed information from the plane back to the mission team. The team used this information to make flight adjustments.

Intelligence analysts then studied the Predator's pictures and video. They identified targets and looked for suspicious activity. They tried to spot any information that might be useful for ground troops.

At the Controls

When flying a Predator the pilot and sensor operator sit side by side in a ground control station. The station is usually housed in a dimly lit trailer. Inside the trailer, the pilot and sensor operator face several computer screens. The upper screen shows a map of the target area and a small plane symbol to show the plane's location. The pilot's lower screen streams

Did You Know?

Although the Predator is pilotless, it takes about 55 crew members on the ground, working in shifts, to operate the UAV during a 24-hour mission.

A team operates a Predator aircraft in Iraq from a ground control station in Nevada.

video from the Predator's nose camera and data from its instruments. These readings tell the pilot how fast the plane is going, how high it is flying, and other flight information.

The pilot uses a flight stick, throttle, and keyboard to control the plane. By moving the flight stick, the pilot can turn the plane, follow a target, or circle over a location. Because the pilot's commands

How a UAV Strike Occurs

There are generally five steps during a UAV strike.

Step 1: Ground units in a war zone request air support from a Predator or a Reaper. Their requests might be to track a vehicle, scan roads for bombs, or provide cover for troops.

Step 2: Once the request is approved, the UAV flight team sends a UAV to the target area.

Step 3: The UAV flies above the target and sends video to ground troops and pilot crews in the United States.

Step 4: The UAV locates the target. The UAV pilot talks to ground troops through a satellite link to determine and identify targets.

Step 5: The UAV marks the target. Then the ground commander gives the OK to strike. The UAV pilot fires the missile while the sensor operator keeps the laser designator's light on the target. Strike complete.

are relayed by satellite, a two-second delay occurs between when he or she tells the plane to turn and when it responds.

Some pilots say that flying the Predator is like looking through a straw. A cockpit pilot uses his or her eyes to see outside the plane. A Predator pilot, however, depends on a video camera to see outside the plane. He or she cannot see as much or as clearly as a cockpit pilot sees. Although this is a disadvantage, it is much safer to be a Predator pilot than it is to be a cockpit pilot.

The sensor operator controls the plane's video and communications equipment, radar, and weapons. He or she focuses on objects on the ground. The sensor operator can also zoom in and out or change the camera's direction.

Some Predators are equipped with laser-guided missiles carried under the aircraft.

Weapons Systems

The Predator has a laser designator that helps missiles from other planes hit targets. The sensor operator tilts and swivels the laser light and fixes it on a target. The laser's path guides missiles to the target.

Some Predators also carry weapons. Two laser-guided Hellfire missiles sit under the wings. To fire the missiles, the mission team fixes the plane's laser on a target and then releases the missiles. The missiles follow the reflected laser energy to the target. They fly at 950 miles per hour (1,529km/h) and can hit a target 5 miles (8km) away.

In a short time UAVs like the Predator have changed the way war is fought. They have also made a difference by keeping soldiers safer.

Chapter 3

UAVs: Making a Difference

UAVs have changed warfare. They have also saved the lives of many pilots and soldiers. One person whose life has changed is Captain Adam Brockshus. He is a pilot stationed at Creech Air Force Base in Nevada. Every day he leaves his home in the Las Vegas suburbs to go to work.

Predator pilots who flew combat missions in Afghanistan from field offices in the United States could still be home in time for dinner with their families.

Fighting the War from Home

Creech Air Force Base is the home of the U.S. Air Force's 432nd Wing. The 432nd flies the air force's Predator and Reaper UAVs. Brockshus learned to fly the Predator at Creech. In a short time he became one of the air force's most experienced Predator pilots. During one mission Brockshus remembers watching a house in the Middle East. The house gave the enemy a lookout over the road. One night Brockshus saw two people stringing wire from the house to the road. The next night his Predator's cameras showed figures crouching beside the road and plugging in the wires. They were creating a roadside bomb. Brockshus relayed the information to nearby troops on the ground. They gave him the okay to fire. Brockshus pushed a

On the Offensive

In November 2002 a sport-utility vehicle (SUV) drove along a winding country road in Yemen. Six men sat inside the vehicle. One man was a senior member of the terrorist group al Qaeda. He had helped plan the attack two years earlier on the battleship USS *Cole* in Yemen. Seventeen Americans were killed during that attack.

Ten thousand feet (3,048m) in the air, a Predator slowly followed the SUV. Some 350 miles (563km) away an American sat at a television screen and watched a video feed of the SUV. With the target identified, the American launched a Hellfire missile from the Predator's wing. The missile streaked toward the desert floor, hitting the target. The SUV exploded in a ball of fire.

The Yemen strike was an important turning point in UAV history. Although it was not the first time a UAV had been used in combat, it was the first time an armed UAV had successfully attacked a high-value target by itself.

An air force pilot operates an MQ-9 Reaper on a training mission at Creech Air Force base in Nevada.

button and launched a missile from his Predator. He watched as the missile destroyed the roadside bomb. Brockshus' actions helped to protect the lives of ground soldiers thousands of miles away.

Captain Brockshus is an example of how UAVs have changed pilots' lives. At work Brockshus flies combat missions around the world. When his shift is over he becomes a dad and husband at home. Today Brockshus trains new pilots to fly the Predator.

Saving Lives

Colonel Pete Gersten's life has also changed because of UAVs. A former fighter jet pilot, he now commands the 432nd Wing at Creech. His fleet of UAVs delivered video from the battlefields in Iraq and Afghanistan without risking his

Did You Know?

Pilots at Creech Air Force Base can operate up to four UAVs at once, allowing them to fly missions in different countries on the same day.

crews' lives. His pilots flew in combat daily.

For a commander like Gersten, keeping his pilots and crews safe has another valuable benefit. Shortly after he took command at Creech, a Predator crashed during a training flight. Gersten stood on the runway and looked at the wreckage. A feeling of deep relief washed over him.

The MQ-9 Reaper

The next generation Predator is called the MQ-9 Reaper. The Reaper is larger and more powerful than the Predator. The Reaper can fly twice as fast. It also flies farther, about 3,600 miles (5,794km), and can soar up to 50,000 feet (15,240m) high. The Reaper is more efficient than the Predator. It can carry ten times the weapons load, including 500-pound (227kg) precision bombs. The Reaper's speed and weapons allow it to quickly locate moving targets that escape a Predator.

The next generation Predator, called the MQ-9 Reaper, is larger, more powerful, and more sophisticated than earlier planes.

Did You Know?

Imagers on the Reaper can read a license plate from 2 miles (3km) away.

He had always dreaded the day he might have to write a letter telling someone's mother and father, or wife, husband, or child, about the loss of an aircraft containing their loved one. The pilotless plane spared him this sad duty.

UAVs in War

UAVs fly several types of missions. Often they gather general intelligence. They spend hours over an area watching and waiting. They report changes in village activity and monitor traffic on roads. In preparation for a raid or a missile strike, the UAV crew may linger over an area for weeks.

Sometimes a UAV will track a suspected enemy. The UAV's cameras record when the suspect goes to work. They watch whom he talks to and where he goes. This constant watching also helps protect innocent lives. If commanders order a strike, the UAV can watch and wait until most **civilians** are out of harm's way.

Other times UAVs watch over ground troops. They warn troops of enemy activity nearby. They spot roadside bombs and warn troops about them. They also help spoil enemy ambushes.

Did You Know?

The Predator's first official name was the RQ-1 Predator. The R stands for reconnaissance, and the Q shows that it is an unmanned aerial vehicle. Armed Predators use the MQ-1 name. The M stands for "multiuse," meaning it is used for both reconnaissance and armed strikes.

UAVs provide close air support during ground operations. They fly overhead and send video to a ground commander's laptop computer. The commanders no longer have to guess what waits beyond the next mountain or bend in the road. They have already seen it. This information is so helpful that many ground commanders will not move forward without it.

During a battle some UAVs fly high and direct other planes. When a plane goes down or soldiers are trapped, UAVs can fly overhead and use their cameras as part of a search-and-rescue mission.

Taking Away Enemy Strengths

Enemy troops often work in secret. They move at night or hide in mountains and valleys. UAVs, however, have taken away much of their secrecy. Infrared cameras and SAR see through pitch-black conditions to reveal the enemy's activity. Circling UAVs see and report on activity in hard-to-reach areas long before ground troops could arrive.

A New Type of Pilot

An air force pilot learns how to control UAVs at Creech Air Force Base in Nevada.

To date, the U.S. Air Force has used pilots already trained on manned planes to fly UAVs. The demand for UAV pilots is so fierce, however, that the air force is currently testing a new type of pilot. It is training a group of Predator pilots who have never flown in a real cockpit. These armchair pilots go through six months of basic flight instruction. Then they head to a nine-week course in combat training at Creech Air Force Base. Growing up with video games, texting, and computers may be an advantage for these new pilots. Gamer skills like following action on multiple screens, instant messaging, and talking to several people at once are used every day by UAV pilots.

The enemy also uses early-warning systems to escape and hide. When they hear helicopters approaching, they take cover. Spies also watch vehicles leave bases and follow them. Warned that troops are coming, the enemy can quickly hide their weapons and pretend to be civilians. Now UAVs follow enemies as they try to hide and pinpoint their location for ground troops. They warn troops which people in the crowd are dangerous, even if they are disguised as civilians.

In 2009, the U.S. Air Force trained more UAV pilots than fighter and bomber pilots. In 2010, the air force plans to buy more UAVs than piloted planes. UAVs are also evolving and expanding into areas outside of the military. In the future pilotless planes will improve many more lives.

Chapter 4

Taking Off in the Future

UAV manufacturers are improving current planes to make them faster and stronger. New UAVs will be better able to protect soldiers' lives. UAVs are also being adapted so they can be used outside the military. They may soon become valuable in many civilian uses.

Did You Know?

UAVs may eventually be used as small tankers to refuel other aircraft in flight.

Military Use Expands

As the Reaper takes flight, GA-ASI is already at work on the Predator C. This UAV, called the Avenger, is the latest version of the Predator. It can fly twice as fast as the Reaper. GA-ASI is also working to make

The Israeli Air Force has developed the UAV Heron, which is being used in the drug war in Central America.

the Avenger **stealthier**. It has made changes to the plane to reduce its radar and **thermal signature**. This would make it more difficult for the enemy to detect the plane. The Avenger is also the first UAV to have an internal weapons bay. Carrying weapons inside makes enemy radar less able to identify the UAV.

Another advancement is to make pilotless planes that are able to fight other UAVs. According to the U.S. Department of Defense, 32 countries are working on over 250 pilotless plane models. In response, U.S. engineers are trying to make a UAV that could fight enemy UAVs. One research program is called the Peregrine UAV Killer. Like a peregrine falcon hunting other birds, this model is designed to circle over an area until it sees an enemy UAV. Then it would dive down and fire at it.

The Raven

The Raven is one of the smallest UAVs currently used in the military. It weighs about 4.5 pounds (2kg) and is only 38 inches (97cm) in length. Small UAVs like the Raven help soldiers on the ground see what waits over the next hill or around the corner. This is handy for spotting ambushes or explosive traps set by the enemy. Troops can easily carry the Raven in three small cases that fit into a backpack.

They can bring a Raven wherever a patrol travels. Troops can launch the Raven by hand in minutes, like a model airplane. It flies automatically if programmed, or an operator can remotely control the plane. Powered by a battery, the Raven can stay in flight for about 45 to 60 minutes. Its cameras allow advance troops to gather information around them without risking the soldiers' lives.

A U.S. soldier prepares an RQ-11 Raven miniature UAV for a reconnaissance mission.

Engineers are also working to make pilotless planes more independent. Future models may be able to repair themselves if disabled. These UAVs may also be able to respond quickly to unexpected threats. If the enemy fires a missile at them, the UAVs could react and destroy the threat on their own.

Other Types of UAV Aircraft

Beyond planes, other aerial vehicles might be used as UAVs. Researchers are working on a glider powered by the sun and liquid hydrogen. The enormous glider's wingspan is almost the length of a football field. It could stay in the air for seven to ten days.

Blimps are another potential UAV aircraft. One company, Lockheed Martin, is developing a high-altitude airship that is 25 times larger than the Goodyear blimp. Flying at an altitude of 100,000 feet (30,480m), these airships could linger for weeks, months, or years. They could act

A Lockheed Martin executive talks about the company's efforts to design a high-altitude blimp for the Missile Defense Agency.

Did You Know?

Armed Reapers can fly over cities hosting the Olympic Games to provide security.

as spy satellites. They could even become floating gas stations for other aircraft.

Micro UAVs

Researchers are also working to find the right technology to shrink the smallest UAVs. In the future, they want to design a micro UAV that could fit comfortably in the palm of the hand. It would be light enough for a soldier to carry in his or her backpack. A micro UAV's small size would give it a big advantage. It would be hard to spot and even harder to shoot down.

A micro UAV would be especially useful in urban areas. It could enter a building before soldiers do to look for hostages or warn of an ambush. It could also send surveillance from dangerous areas after a chemical weapons attack.

One micro UAV in development is called the Robofly. This tiny machine weighs only .002 ounces (57mg) and has a 1.2-inch (3cm) wingspan. One day soldiers may send out a team of Roboflies to find targets or search for chemical and biological weapons.

Public Safety

In the future, UAVs also may be used in many noncombat roles. U.S. Coast Guard

UAVs could perform search-and-rescue missions and patrol the coasts. Police departments could use UAVs in many ways. UAV cameras could monitor large crowds. Using a face recognition program, UAVs could identify a suspect and follow him or her. Police could also use a UAV to stake out a suspect's house. Officers would then know what dangers awaited before they entered for an arrest. UAVs could also track gang activity or take pictures of crime scenes. Traffic cops could fly UAVs to learn about road congestion and accidents.

Fire departments are already discovering the value of UAVs. The planes can quickly reach and scan remote areas to pinpoint where a fire is burning. UAVs can also fly over large forest fires and send back information to firefighters. During one large California fire, a UAV flew over the area for sixteen hours. It took pictures that helped firefighters see the dangerous fire's edge.

The U.S. Customs and Border Protection Agency also plans to use more Predator planes to patrol borders. These planes can monitor areas that are hard to reach

Researchers are working to shrink the size of UAVs to palm-sized micro flyers.

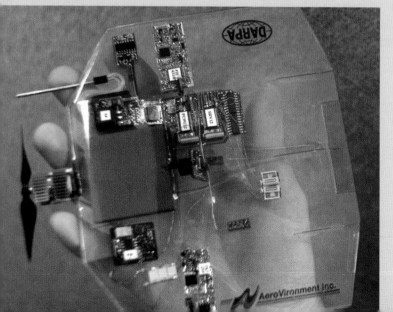

on the ground. At night infrared cameras spot drug smugglers and illegal aliens sneaking over the border. One night agent Dave Gasho watched a video feed from a Predator patrolling the border. He spotted five men carrying large, heavy backpacks north of the border. He radioed a nearby helicopter to fly to the area. When the men heard the helicopter, they tried to hide, but the Predator's cameras followed them. Gasho beamed the Predator's laser on their hiding spot. The helicopter team followed the laser and arrested the suspects, who were carrying illegal drugs.

Working with the Environment

UAV cameras and sensors may be used to protect and study the environment as well. When an oil pipeline breaks, UAVs could quickly find the break and direct repair crews. Instead of sending people to assess toxic chemical spills, UAVs could fly in and gather the information safely.

Studying Flies

Scientists are studying flies in hopes of unlocking the secrets of insect flight. They hope that understanding how flies fly will help them design tiny, insectlike UAVs. A company called Cognition for Technical Systems is working on a flight simulator for flies. It hopes that analyzing a fly's brain during flight will help the company design a micro UAV navigation system. Other researchers are looking at how fly wings work. They are using this information to design a tiny flapping-wing UAV that could better maneuver in close, indoor spaces.

Tracking Pirates

The Indian Ocean off the coast of Somalia is often filled with modern-day pirates. These pirates attack ships in the area, taking goods and hostages. Ships full of oil, coal, or other goods can bring in millions of dollars for a daring pirate. As a result, piracy is increasing in the area. To combat the pirates, Reaper UAVs are being sent into the airspace above the Indian Ocean. A Reaper will patrol the ocean and search for pirates. When it spots a suspicious ship, the Reaper's crew will warn other ships in the area to stay clear. They will also work with naval vessels to target and stop the pirate ships before they can attack.

A U.S. Navy vessel launches a Scan-Eagle UAV as part of an effort to track pirate activity off the coast of Somalia.

Meteorologists can also use UAVs. Because there is no pilot risk, UAVs can gather weather and storm information in dangerous places. They could monitor cyclones, volcanic eruptions, and other weather events. Researchers have flown a small UAV into the middle of a tropical storm. The UAV entered the storm only a few hundred feet above water, where the winds and conditions were the fiercest. UAVs may also be used to fly over the ocean and drop devices to measure ocean temperatures.

UAVs can also track and gather information on the world's animals. From the air, UAVs can easily identify and count animals. Through UAV videos, researchers watch animals without disturbing them. Hard-to-see nighttime activity becomes clear on infrared cameras. In 2008, a group of Australian marine scientists began testing a small UAV to count and photograph **dugongs** and humpback whales off the Queensland coast.

Commercial Uses

UAVs may also change life for fishermen and farmers. UAVs could fly over the ocean searching for **shoals** of fish. Then they could direct fishing boats toward the fish. UAVs flying over farmland could send back pictures and video to help farmers assess the health of their crops. In Hawaii farmers can send a UAV over coffee fields. The plane identifies which fields are ripe for picking. In addition, UAVs might eventually be equipped to spray farmlands with pesticides and fertilizers.

Did You Know?

UAVs are currently highly restricted in civilian airspace. In order to allow them to fly safely with manned planes, new air traffic control systems based on electronic communications need to be developed.

Some people think that UAVs may be used for commercial airline flights in the future. It is most likely that cargo flights would be the first to use pilotless planes. Eventually though, almost any type of airplane may be adapted for pilotless flight.

In only a few years, pilotless planes changed the military. As design and technology improve, these planes will become smarter, faster, and easier to control. They have the potential to impact and improve many areas of life. Someday UAVs may replace all piloted planes. Pilotless planes are ready to soar to the top of aviation for years to come.

Glossary

avionics: The science and technology of electrical and electronic devices in flight.

civilians: People who are not in active duty with a military, police, or firefighting unit.

combat: Armed fighting with enemy forces.

drone: A pilotless aircraft operated by remote control.

dugongs: Marine mammals found in the Red Sea and the Indian Ocean that have a barrel-shaped body, flipperlike forelimbs, no hind limbs, and a triangular tail.

epoxy resin: A high-strength glue.

infrared: Light that cannot be seen by the human eye.

intelligence analysts: People who gather and study information about an enemy.

meteorologists: Scientists who study and report on the weather and climate.

reconnaissance: A search for useful military information.

satellite: A device that is launched into orbit around Earth.

shoals: Large schools of fish.

stealthier: Acting quieter and with more secrecy to avoid notice.

surveillance: A watch kept over a person, group, or place.

thermal signature: The temperature of an object that exceeds that of its environment.

For More Information

Books

Michael and Gladys Green, *Remotely Piloted Aircraft: The Predators*. Mankato, MN: Capstone, 2004. Written for kids, this book discusses the most famous UAV—the Predator.

Larry Hama and Bill Cain, *Unmanned Aerial Vehicles*. Danbury, CT: Children's, Press 2007. This book gives basic information about UAVs, how they are used, and different types of UAVs.

Web Sites to Visit

General Atomics Aeronautical Systems, Incorporated (www.ga-asi.com). This Web site gives detailed descriptions of the Predator and Reaper systems. It also includes press releases and news coverage of the Predator and Reaper UAVs.

National Museum of the U.S. Air Force (www.nationalmuseum.af.mil). This Web site gives information on the history and planes of the U.S. Air Force. The Modern Flight Gallery (Exhibits section) includes fact sheets on the Predator, Reaper, and Global Hawk UAVs.

NOVA: **Spies That Fly** (www.pbs.org/wgbh/nova/spiesfly). This Web site, which is part of PBS, has transcripts from the *NOVA* special on pilotless planes as well as timelines of UAV history and examples of radar pictures sent from UAVs.

Index

A
Animals, 43
Avenger (Predator C),
  35–36

B
Blimps, 38–39
Brockshus, Adam, 26–29

C
Coast Guard, U.S., 39–40
Combat, 5, 26–27
Corona spy satellite, 13
Customs and Border
  Protection Agency, U.S.,
  40–41

D
Department of Defense,
  U.S., 10–11, 36

F
Flies, 41

G
Gasho, Dave, 41

General Atomics
  Aeronautical Systems,
  Incorporated (GA-ASI),
  11, 15, 35
Gersten, Pete, 29, 31
Gliders, 38
Global Hawk, 14, 21
Global positioning
  system (GPS), 11, 19
Gulf War, 8–9

H
Hellfire missiles, 14

I
Infrared cameras, 4

L
Laser designators, 14
Lightning Bug, 8
Lockheed Martin, 38

M
MQ-9 Reaper, 4, 30,
  35

P
Peregrine UAV Killer, 36
Pilots, 20, 22–24, 33
  numbers trained, 34
Pioneer, 8–10
Predator drones, 4–6, 11–
  12
  cameras on, 4, 12,
    18–19
  construction of, 16–17
  cost of, 14
  ease of transporting, 17
  endurance of, 15
  laser targeting by, 14
  official names of, 32
  operators controlling,
    20, 22
  speed of, 10
  weapons systems of, 25
  weight of, 16
  wingspan of, 20

R
Raven, 37
Robofly, 39

S
Synthetic aperture radar
  (SAR), 19, 32

U
Unmanned aerial vehicles
  (UAV), 5–7
  commercial uses of,
    43–44
  Israeli innovations in,
    8
  micro, 39
  models in use, 14
  public safety uses for,
    39–41
  steps in strike by, 24
  in tracking pirates, 42
  type of missions flown
    by, 31–32

V
Vietnam War, 8

W
Weather, 43

Picture Credits

Cover: AP Images
AFP/Getty Images, 36, 37
AP Images, 12, 13, 18 (right), 25, 30, 33, 38, 40, 42
© Bettmann/Corbis, 6 (right), 9

Christian Science Monitor/Getty Images, 26
Dave Gatley/MAI/Landov, 23
Getty Images, 5, 6 (left), 7, 16, 17, 18 (left), 28
UPI/Northrop Grumman/Landov, 21
USMC/MAI/Landov, 11

About the Author

Carla Mooney is the author of several books for young adults and children. She lives in Pittsburgh, Pennsylvania with her husband and three children.